EXPLORING CONSCIOUS ENERGY

A LOGICAL APPROACH TO PARANORMAL INVESTIGATION

BRIAN KENT

Book Layout ©2013 BookDesignTemplates.com

Ordering Information:
Quantity sales. Special discounts are available on quantity purchases by corporations, associations, and others. For details, contact the "Special Sales Department" at the address above.

Exploring Conscious Energy/ Brian Kent -- 1st ed.

INTRODUCTION

The goal of this book is to further educate determined paranormal investigators who wish to become more effective and successful in their assistance to others, to open their minds to scientific explanation and to expand their study of the phenomena known as paranormal activity.

There are many techniques and theories in this field, which divert many investigators in various directions. Some are beneficial to both the client and the investigator, while other radical and extreme inclinations seem to miss the mark. The intent of this book is to keep an investigation centered and grounded in fact not fiction.

A true investigator looks for answers, paranormal or not. The truth and facts are nothing more or less than what they are. One must uphold a high degree of integrity by being truthful to oneself and the client, by using solid fact-based judgment in all determinations. This what makes a legitimate investigator.

It is imperative for one to be a skeptic first, making it a priority to approach each investigation agnostically, with the sole intent of finding logical explanations. In other words, the location needs to prove itself to be active. If not, half of the investigation is left untouched–the half which may provide the answers we seek. In order for anyone to be effective in this field, they must be an all-around investigator before pursuing paranormal conclusions.

Therefore, this book is an attempt to encompass all possible facets of an investigation from a logical standpoint, and to better prepare investigators for what lies ahead.

ONE

MOTIVATION

Most people believe paranormal investigation is about ghost hunting. Even though seeking confirmation of a human energy presence is part of the process, it is so much more. It is a study of ourselves, our perceptions, our beliefs, mother nature's input, basic science, how human energy exists in this world's equation and what effect and contributions mankind has upon it. Since we are all students of this phenomena, we must remain open-minded to all scientific possibilities and equations. It is my belief, this world has many untapped mysteries which have yet to be discovered.

Paranormal investigation can leave a life changing impression on an investigator. The study and numerous experiences surrounding actual paranormal activity can eventually have an effect on a person's opinion of mortality.

Many of today's investigators have been influenced by the blitz of paranormal reality programs on television. The success of these programs has become a double edged sword. On one side, they have become a support group for many who have yet to come out of the shadows. By raising awareness of a topic which has been swept under the carpet for hundreds of years, these programs have literally put an end to the "dark ages mentality" normally attributed to ghosts.

On the other hand, some of these programs display the topic in dark and mysterious portrayals to attract horror fans and maintain ratings. By doing so, the awareness becomes counterproductive by coloring it in overly exaggerated depictions with the intent to frighten, as opposed to understanding.

It has been my observation that this very same approach to programming applies to investigators as well. There are those who are looking to be frightened and there are those who choose to understand. There are those who **only** seek ghosts and paranormal alternatives, while others are willing to take it a step further by discovering the truth, whether it is paranormal or not. The difference between the two is almost black and white.

With that being said, one must honestly ask...

"What is my main motivation?"

The commercial exploitation of the afterlife is nothing new. It's been going on for centuries and is still going on to this day. Due to the current interest in ghost hunting, we now have paranormal destinations we can visit for a nominal fee. Primarily, these paranormal "hot beds of activity" are designed specifically for personal entertainment not for answers or resolution. Some have guided tours while others actually rent the property for a one night stay. Since these pay-to-investigate destinations are promoting paranormal activity, they provide the entire experience **without the obligations and responsibility** essential to private residential investigations. For those who have a passing interest in this field, who are looking at ghost hunting as a hobby or who wish to produce an independent film or television program, these destinations are a perfect match.

EXPLORING CONSCIOUS ENERGY

However, discreet investigations for a private individual are an entirely different level. Private paranormal investigations have never been about personal agenda or as a form of entertainment even though some thrill seekers tend to differ. It is about discovery and helping those who are experiencing activity in their home or business by placing the client's concerns above the investigator's desire to capture apparitions in action.

For those who are getting into paranormal investigation for answers, discovery, and the will to help others, they will find the many levels of private investigation very rewarding. There is a personal fulfillment and sense of pride in assisting those with paranormal concerns. Investigators with this type of mind set are usually driven by a past experience which has gone unanswered and a true passion for discovery. These cases require a serious, logical approach and a passionate interest to help others.

When taking on the responsibility of a private home or business, an investigator will readily detect the deep concern and genuine fear a client is experiencing. Not only does the investigator have to examine the activity at the location, they have to focus on the client. The investigator may be asked questions which have yet to be answered through the investigation. The investigator may be asked to remove "whatever" is in the location. The client may have certain beliefs which contradict what the investigation has uncovered. The only way to thoroughly examine these cases is through an accurate, factual, and honest investigation of the property. Staying true to oneself and the facts shows respect for the client, the reliability of the team, and regard for the investigation itself.

Why is this so important?

The client is counting on professional etiquette and an accurate determination of their property. If an investigator can find logical cause(s) for a client's claims, the case can be solved. If a team can provide factual evidence supporting paranormal activity, most clients are willing to accept the verdict, therefore opening their minds to possible solutions. The main objective is to answer the clients biggest question– "Is my property haunted or not?" It is an investigator's responsibility to answer that to the best of their ability.

Understanding one's motivation for this field should be a top priority. If one is not mentally prepared or in the right mind set for private investigation, an investigator will soon be in deep water. Mishandled cases can take on serious ramifications. The case can become counterproductive to a client, make matters worse at the location, and destroy any prior credibility the investigator(s) may have had. Know yourself, be truthful with yourself, know your intentions, understand the responsibilities, and be fully prepared for the task at hand.

T W O

WHAT ARE GHOSTS?

Mankind has questioned, theorized, debated, and scrutinized the existence of ghosts for centuries. Researchers, who do believe there is a metaphysical makeup for these beings, loosely base their explanations on what we do know about conservative energy and electromagnetic fields.

In 2008, I posted a theory which attempts to connect the dots between Einstein's Law of Conservative Energy and the bio-electrical energy existing in our body. This is my hypothesis.

The Theory of Conscious Energy
Brian Kent/2008

Throughout the in utero period, atoms develop cells, which in turn develop a brain, due to our DNA makeup. Throughout the process, the brain becomes our main contributor to cellular growth. In order to do that, the brain requires the assistance of these atoms to provide it with a power supply. These atoms are the energy source a physical being will require throughout its physical existence. Atoms consist of protons which produce a positive charge, neutrons which have a neutral charge and

5

electrons which carry a negative charge. The brain distributes this energy through the nervous system via neurons to promote cellular growth, the development of organs and standard physical operation. The amount of energy produced by the human body is between 10 and 100 millivolts of bio-electricity (enough to power a 25 watt light bulb). The brain uses up approximately 20% of this current to keep the body functioning and for its own processes and development.

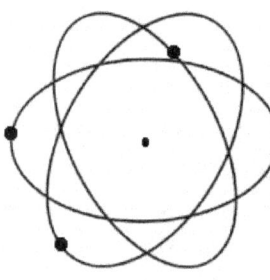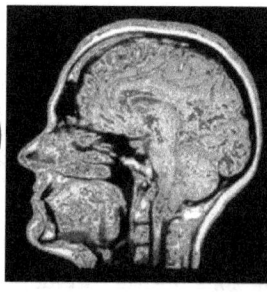

Since our body is primarily made up of water, it acts as a conductor for the energy it contains. When current flows through a conductor, it develops a magnetic resonant field pattern in and around the body or what is called an electromagnetic field. All physical beings produce these patterns outside of their bodily confines which can be influenced by external magnetic fields, such as other living organisms, electronic devices, and the Earth's own electromagnetic field. The human brain can produce a field several feet from the head, which some call the human aura. The electrical charges from a human brain can be measured using an EEG proving humans do, in fact, carry their own electromagnetic field. As a result, the human body can act as an aerial which has the potential for simultaneous transmission and reception of energy within its environment. Judging by this analysis, human consciousness is theoretically a quantifiable phenomena and partially measurable as an electromagnetic energy radiating outside of its bodily limitations.

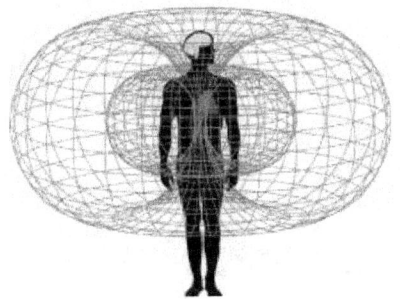

Establishing our energy source and its capabilities is crucial to this theory, especially if energy is considered indestructible. The Law of Conservative Energy states "energy may neither be created or destroyed. Therefore the sum of all energies in the system remains constant." Einstein's theory went on to suggest "energy cannot be destroyed, but is transformed."

Attaching consciousness to the energy in our body may be as simple as reading this book. The largest consumer of our energy is the brain. As we go through life our brain acts as a hard drive on a computer, storing thoughts and ideas, things we have learned, experiences, emotions, reactions and beliefs which are assembled into our personality. Like all organs the brain is mortal, but as energy flows through the brain's neurons storing personal data, this hypothesis suggests, the energy itself may be simultaneously absorbing consciousness into its electromagnetic field, thus coupling the two together.

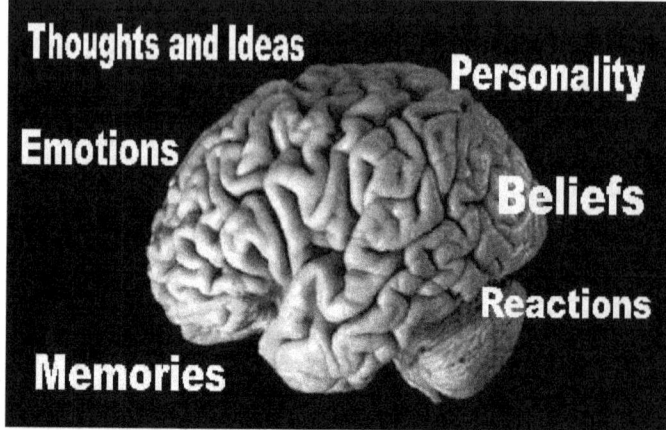

The transformation phase from a physical state to a state of conscious energy relies on what we know of the Earth's electromagnetic field. We do know the Earth's field is approximately 0.5 gauss. A physical being's EMF is much less and measured in milligauss units.

This theory suggests the atoms in our body are identical to the Earth's, therefore the magnetic fields are compatible. Since the Earth's field is much greater, it simply reintegrates our magnetic field (with our consciousness intact) back into its own once our body is no longer able to sustain it. This would, in theory, maintain "the sum of all energies in the system."

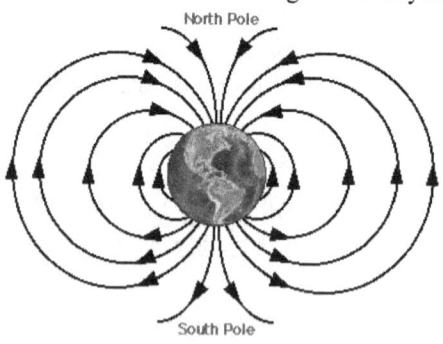

EXPLORING CONSCIOUS ENERGY

If this hypothesis stands correct, our consciousness would be able to identify our change in embodiment and existence, making it intelligent. Since magnetic fields are capable of manipulating each other, it would seem conscious energy would be able to learn how to operate in an electromagnetic state. If so, conscious energy could be capable of causing EMF disruption, drawing energy from the environment and other sources, manipulating electrical devices, invading radio waves or frequencies, moving things by working magnetic poles against each other, transmitting a verbal response through the EM field and possibly invading the subconscious of other living beings. All of which is considered paranormal activity.

For a period of time, our atomic makeup forms a complicated organism which we identify as the human body. The current in our body fuels the brain which stores our personality providing this energy source with intelligence and an identity. Upon the body's passing, the magnetic field our body produced is reintegrated back into the Earth's magnetic field with our consciousness still intact. Hypothetically, this conscious energy disbursement is what we consider a ghost.

THREE

EQUIPMENT

Over the past century, investigators have used less than advanced methods and tools which were not very reliable sources to base evidence upon. Most equipment used today provides some degree of measure and is used by scientists, home inspectors, electricians, plumbers and professional contractors. The benefit of most these devices is their dual purpose use. They can assist an investigator during a preliminary home inspection as well as a detection device.

When first starting out it's easy to get caught up in purchasing all the latest equipment. Some have outrageous claims of operation. Some are just duplicates of others. Some combine numerous features in an all-in-one package.

It's important to decide what we are capable of understanding and operating. Researching the equipment in advance and asking questions allows us to understand what we are buying and how it will benefit our investigations. Attending conventions or other group meetings, enables to physically analyze the equipment prior to purchase.

EXPLORING CONSCIOUS ENERGY

There are scams in the paranormal marketplace, so buyer beware. If an item sounds too good to be true, it probably is. If an individual or dealer has been rumored or proven to be less than reputable, it may be best to consider an alternative source of purchase.

When buying equipment, we must consider accessories which may be required to make our purchases operational. Some devices are not fully equipped with everything we need. Read up on connections (cords, USB chords, channel cable, etc.) and what kind of media to purchase, (tapes, discs, memory cards) chargers, batteries, tripods, etc. If we do our research, we will have everything we need when the time comes to use it.

The prime directive of any investigation is to gather proof and the truth. The only way to collect that kind of evidence is through the equipment being used, the knowledge of the equipment, the readings gathered from the equipment, and documentation through audio, video or photographic means. They are the foundation of the case.

Video, Audio, Photographic

The top of the list is a decent hand held **digital camcorder with night vision.** It is usually preferred to have one with a flip out screen and the steady shot option to lessen the jolted movement often attributed to hand help operation. If it takes a memory card, find out what kind of cards are out there and their storage capabilities. If it takes tape, research specs and availability.

Digital Camcorder with Night Vision

Digital cameras with a flash are a must. Research the camera's picture quality standards, auto focus options, and if it is capable of being mounted on a tripod. Many investigators are using full-spectrum digital cameras which allow UV and IR light in during the photo process. This is considered a specialty item, so do research and chose carefully. Always look into the accessories, memory cards, and if external full spectrum illumination is needed.

Digital Camera and Full Spectrum Illuminator

Digital Voice recorders are essential in any investigation and are required to capture EVP's or Electronic Voice Phenomena. There are numerous brands and price ranges making it possible to conform to any budget. Some supply the software and accessories to make downloads easy. Some investigators still use analog voice recorders which require a tape. Sound quality does suffer due to a lack of digital performance, therefore fresh tape is recommended.

Analog and Digital Voice Recorders

DVR Night Vision Surveillance Units are not completely necessary, but are considered primary equipment due to their provision of numerous video angles which supply a greater amount of documentation. Some have a capability to monitor and record sixteen locations at once. When considering a budget, be aware that DVR units may require a monitor and other equipment.

8 Channel Surveillance Unit

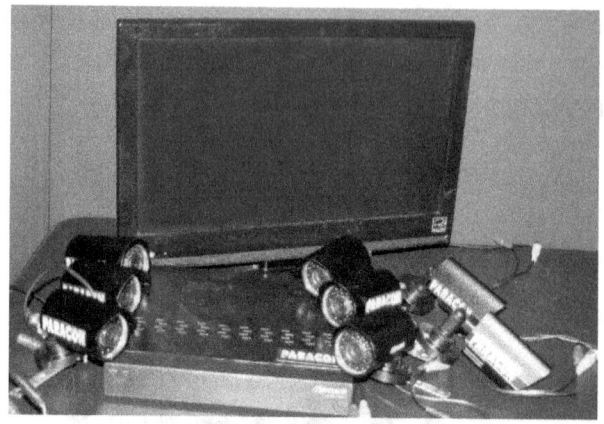

Detection Devices

Investigators use various detection devices to capture environmental readings. These devices are utilized in both the preliminary and paranormal aspects of their research. In practical application, these devices can notify an investigator of EMF radiation from electronics and unshielded wiring, drafts from insufficient seals or insulation, poor air quality, complications due to sound frequency and carbon monoxide infiltration, to name a few. When used genuinely and properly, they can offer factual solutions to a clients claims. In relation to paranormal research, these devices allegedly detect environmental changes brought on by paranormal disturbances. All of these devices come in various forms and price ranges. The following is a collection of the most notable.

The **KII Meter** is the EMF detector most associated with paranormal investigation. It's one of the most popular models and reasonably priced. Although not very decimal point accurate in its readings, it can provide a rough estimate in the severity and reach of EMF radiation.

KII Meter

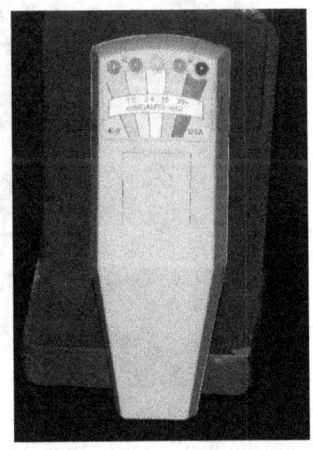

The **Tri-Field Meter** is capable of measuring AC magnetic, AC electric and radio waves. The three-axis Tri-field Meter's main selling point is its capability to measure the true strength of these three fields, regardless of which way it is pointed. Therefore, the Trifield Meter can be scanned rapidly across an area without having to stop at each point to search for a maximum reading. The **Natural Tri-Field Meter** detects natural DC fields. It's high sensitivity to natural EM fields makes it a preference in paranormal research.

Tri-Field Natural EM Meter

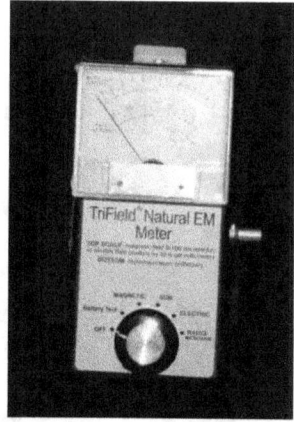

The **Mel-Meter** is a jack-of-all-trades. All models have EMF detection and ambient temperature readings displayed on a lit screen. Some come with a vibration sensor, some with an EMF radiating antenna, some with REM Pod features and some include hot and cold spot alarms. There is a model for every budget.

Mel Meter

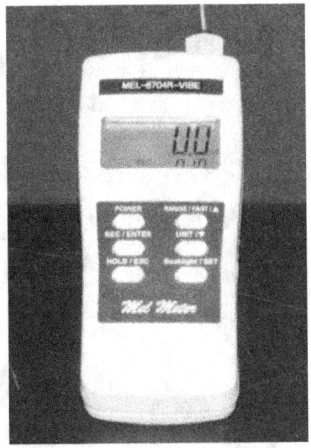

The **EMF Data Logger** can be used as a standard hand held EMF detector or as a stationary post, recording level changes over periods of time, time stamping spikes, then saving it's documentation for later analysis. If multiple units are lined up in succession, EMF data loggers can determine time, distance, and direction of a moving EM field.

EMF Data Logger

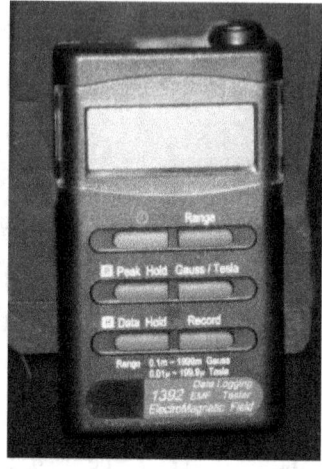

REM Pods are designed for stationary posts. By positioning them in an active area and extending the antenna, these pods produce a radiant EM field of their own. If a stray or moving electromagnetic field invades the pod's emitted field, an alarm will go off with lights indicating the external field's rough proximity and intensity.

REM Pod

EXPLORING CONSCIOUS ENERGY

Drastic temperature changes are often attributed to drafts, vent placement and other practical applications. However, cold spots which defy description may be considered paranormal. For this very reason, an **IR Thermometer** is considered a necessity. It's digital read-out provides ambient room temperature and laser pinpoint readings for specific spots once the trigger is squeezed.

IR thermometer

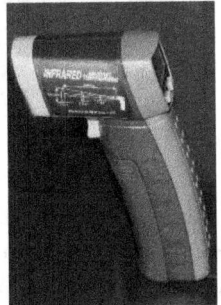

One of the most costly and highly sought after pieces of equipment is the **Thermal Imaging Infrared Camera.** Infrared detection and simultaneous temperature readings produce thermal images in specified colors and shapes. IR vision makes it very handy in dark locations and its ability to provide a visual representation of temperature change puts it in a league of its own.

IR Thermal Imaging Camera

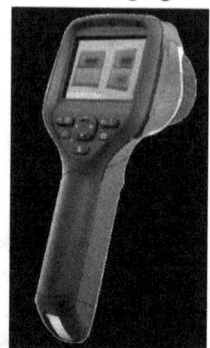

Motion sensors have become a common tool in most investigations. Considered unreliable in outdoor settings, they have their moments, detecting unaccounted movement indoors. It is recommended purchasing these sensors with an alarm which can immediately notify the team of said occurrences.

Motion Sensors

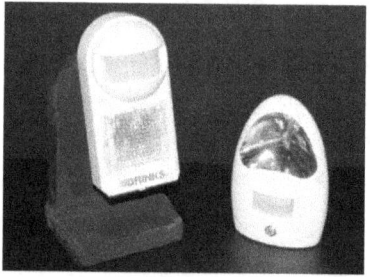

Trap cameras have proven to be fairly reliable. They have a motion sensor built inside which triggers a camera to take a photo or a one minute video, depending on the setting. They require a memory card which mounts inside the unit, saving the camera's data for download.

Hunters Trap Camera

Baby Monitors are useful while monitoring a one-on-one EVP session, and at base in correlation with surveillance, when audio is not available.

Baby Monitor

Shadow Detectors are designed to be used with a laser making direct contact with its internal eye. If anything breaks the lasers contact with the eye an alarm is triggered notifying team members of the occurrence.

Shadow Detector

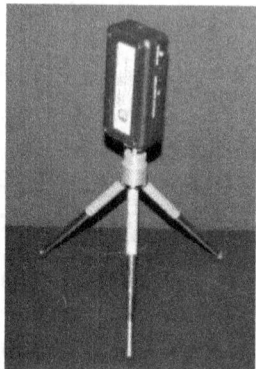

Specific & Advanced Devices

Infrared Illuminators are exactly what the name implies. They enhance night vision video production by increasing and extending the reach of infrared illumination. They are perfect for shots down long hallways, large rooms, and outdoors.

IR Illuminator

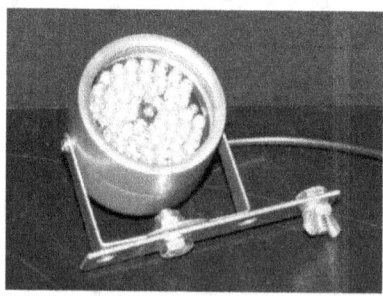

It is believed shadows and black masses are capable of blocking light. **Laser Grids** provide that light. Green pen lasers are designed to cast thousands of pin lights against a wall making it seemingly impossible to pass in front of without detection. Red block lasers produce a grid just as impassable with the added capability to define shape and dimension.

Laser Grid Pen

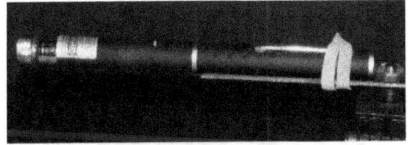

The infamous **Ghost Box** or Frank's Box is an AM/FM radio which has been modified to rapidly scan radio frequencies without the capability of locking into one channel. It is believed an entity can use the radio waves and white noise between the channels to communicate with the living. Considering these devices are subject to radio signals, the verdict is still out regarding their accuracy. However, the **RT-EVP** real time voice recorder has an FM scanning feature which records while it scans numerous air waves per second. This feature provides the white noise needed, while drastically minimizing the chances of radio station interference.

RT-EVP Unit

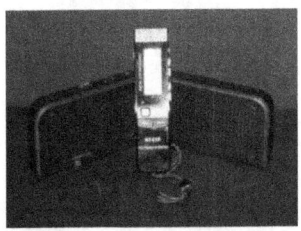

Barometric readings are starting to become standard practice amongst investigators. **Hand Held Barometers** are finding their way into more investigations in an attempt to retrieve extensive environmental data surrounding paranormal activity. Many models include temperature and humidity indicators, as well. Since they are inexpensive, informative, easy to operate, small and mobile, barometers are an excellent accessory.

Barometer / Altimeter

A **Carbon Monoxide Detector** is one piece of equipment all investigators should have on hand. Carbon monoxide is an odorless gas which can cause dizziness, headaches, nausea, health problems, mental confusion and / or hallucinations which a client could mistake as paranormal activity. This deadly gas is a danger to anyone exposed to it, making these detectors the first piece of equipment used during the preliminary inspection of the property.

Carbon Monoxide Detector

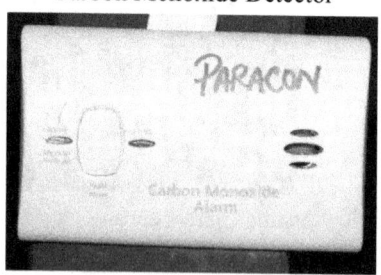

Geophones or vibration sensors are designed to detect the slightest palpitations. They are normally used when claims include footsteps and or items being moved or shaken. The sensitivity is adjustable, making it simple to regulate in various surroundings. Once a disturbance has been detected, a lit display will silently announce the smallest tremor.

Geophone

For investigators who are serious about environmental readings, the **Air Ion Counter** is an excellent way to gather air quality data. It is useful in determining a client's exposure to excessive amounts of positive ions due to smoke, pollen, allergens and other pollutants which have a negative effect on humans, thus making these counters valuable during a preliminary. Some investigators believe the existence of paranormal activity can alter the ion count by boosting positive ion levels in a concentrated area.

Ion Counter

Ever since Vic Tandy discovered the effects of infrasound frequency, **Oscilloscopes** have become quite effective.

Infrasound can be associated with so many paranormal symptoms, making these meters very useful in determining what is or is not paranormal.

Oscilloscope

For those who are not familiar with these correlations, we will be discussing Mr. Tandy's discovery in the following pages.

FOUR

PRELIMINARY INVESTIGATION

I t is very easy to succumb to the power of suggestion. When a client comes to us with claims and stories of paranormal activity, it can be an investigator's natural inclination to jump to a paranormal conclusion, before the investigation has started.

It's important to break this cycle of thought when entering a case.

A client is depending on our voice of reason...not to follow their lead.

Unsubstantiated conclusions can prejudice our judgment and cause us to miss key pieces of evidence, which won't be helping the client. This is why we need to conduct and follow the three steps of a preliminary investigation.

Client Interview:

Most investigations start with some form of contact from a potential client. Usually this contact is made via phone, email, chat on a social page or messaging through a website. The initial claims come in various narrations and description.

Some are vague and fairly standard. Some clients choose to elaborate with colorful metaphors and description believing it will entice a team into an investigation. Some prefer to self-diagnose their experiences, which are obviously influenced by paranormal programming and horror films. There are even a chosen few who go as far as to say their life is in great danger. Again, we are dealing with human nature, how people perceive things differently and the varied ways one may deal with their own fears.

This is where visual images and the power of suggestion need to be shackled, allowing the investigation to find the answers.

Once a client has made first contact, the next step is to set up an appointment to meet with the client at their location. **It is strongly recommended** that two or more investigators attend this meeting for safety reasons. By conducting the client interview at the location, investigator(s) can get a visual prospective of the circumstances and possibly gather more intimate details surrounding each claim.

It is important for the interviewer to keep the client on point. Each claim needs to be addressed separately, gathering as many details as possible which pertain to that particular claim.

Once the information of each claim has been covered, an interviewer should make an attempt to collect personal information about the client and other occupants in the location. This must be done diplomatically, as some people may find it personal or offensive. It can be beneficial to know of any medical conditions or mental issues. Is anyone using prescription drugs? What are they? It can be helpful to understand the home environment. Is it a happy home? Is anyone going through depression, personality changes, mood swings, new habits? Have there been any recent renovations completed or still in the process? Are there any new additions to the location? A baby, an adopted pet, antiques? Has the client been experimenting with Ouija boards, séances, etc.? Are there any religious or spiritual beliefs we should be aware of?

One of the first suspects in any case can be deceased relatives, loved ones, friends, associates, or even acquaintances. A list should be compiled of departed individuals who may have circumstantial bearing on the case. Any one of them may lead the investigation on a course of intent.

Finally, historical data needs to be collected on the location itself. Property owners should have a copy of the abstract or listing of all property owners once the land was developed. It is from this information that research can begin.

Research:

Sometimes a location's history can speak volumes. Historical research is not only fascinating, it may provide important clues to the case. One of the most important documents to research is the **abstract.** If the abstract is fairly accurate and predates any structural development, the list of previous property owners may hold a key. An abstract will also display a property's turnover rate, which may be a clue in itself.

From this list of names, a researcher may want to access the **public census bureau** (if available) which goes a step further by listing **ALL occupants actually living on the property during different time periods.** Since land owners may not have actually lived on the property due to rental or leasing agreements, it is important to know who actually inhabited the property. Knowing these individuals, family members, their age groups, their occupations and how long they resided at the location can produce an entirely different perspective on lifestyle, wealth and stature. Unfortunately, some census records in different areas may be lost or have been destroyed. If fortunate enough to have these listings, they should be put to good use.

Local libraries are another excellent source for historical data. If a library has an extensive collection in their newspaper archives, a researcher may be able to dig up some very interesting facts surrounding a location and its inhabitants. Obituaries may produce information regarding cause of death, grave sites, names of relatives or associates, some of whom may still be alive and available for interview. By searching the address of the location, a researcher may find a news article reporting a tragedy such as a fire, natural disaster, or criminal activity, which may have some degree of significance. By searching specific names, public records may provide a birth or wedding announcement. A researcher may even discover articles on specific individuals which could range from civic achievement to murder. Never underestimate the power of the press and the reported word.

Finally, a must stop is the **local historical society.** If any relevant previous occupants, were upstanding citizens in the community, they will be duly acknowledged in these institutions. If the property itself had historical significance, it may be listed. Historical societies tend to document a region's history, many going back to our country's Native American roots. Their research may provide insight on community traditions, annual activities, political climate or concealed reports of mob activity, KKK involvement, local cults, and secret organizations.

These four resources are an excellent point of reference. In our search for intent, the past may be able to supply an answer.

Research is not only limited to historical data. Using the information gathered from the client interview, a researcher may be called upon to conduct research on the client. A researcher may want to "Google" a client's name for any on-line information from web and social sites. If medical conditions, mental issues or prescriptions have been verified through the interview, it can be useful to know the cause and symptoms of these conditions plus the prescription's benefits and side effects. If the interview reveals religious or spiritual beliefs, it may be useful to gather information on the client's faith and convictions. If the client has introduced a second hand item, artifact or antique into the location which seems to coincide with the activity, a researcher should look into its origins and/or previous owners.

Preliminary Location Inspection:

This is quite possibly the most important part of the preliminaries and is literally an elementary home inspection. With so many contributing factors, a team needs to be diligent in its efforts to uncover all possibilities **before** considering paranormal conclusions.

A great place to start is with an EMF sweep. Electromagnetic fields which are generated by man-made objects, can have an effect on humans. Since we have an electromagnetic field of our own, our bodies can be sensitive to electronics, appliances, unshielded wiring, circuit breakers, large radio towers, power lines, etc. Symptoms include a feeling of being watched, hair standing on end, goose bumps, uneasiness, and in some extreme cases, hallucinations, skin irritation or rashes. Electromagnetic radiation sensitivity is fairly common, especially in older homes with unshielded wiring and in cases where clients are in close proximity to electronics for long periods of time.

To properly conduct an EMF sweep, **slowly** scan the walls and around electronics with an EMF detector. Normal acceptable readings are between 0.0 and 3.0. If a significant spike occurs, slowly move the detector up, down and away from the wall or electronic device to measure its reach and circumference. If the spike is consistent and steady, then it is more than likely wiring in the wall or the electronic device. Once that determination has been made, make note of it and continue. Take a quick look outside the location for any radio or cell phone towers and power lines which may be close by. Document and report all findings to the team.

After the EMF sweep has been completed, temperature and air quality readings are the next step in the process. A location can be exposing a client to many unhealthy but invisible elements which may be effecting them unknowingly. We all know the health risks behind carbon monoxide poisoning, but we should also take into account radon exposure, chemical fumes, excessive allergens and pollen, mold, asbestos, forms of decay, etc. All of these elements can produce air quality issues which could trigger nausea, migraines, hallucinations, skin rashes or accumulative health complications which could lead to death. If a carbon monoxide detector is available, it should be left running throughout the preliminary. If an ion counter is available, a sweep should be conducted of the entire premises, paying close attention to visible areas of concern such as water heaters, furnaces, gas ovens, chemicals, gas lines, chipping paint, mold, forms of decay, etc. Significant steady spikes in the **positive** ion count surrounding these concerns should be duly noted and reported to the client and to the team.

Gathering a location's base temperature reading is a standard practice during a preliminary. By using the ambient setting on a digital thermometer, maneuver from room to room, acknowledging door, window and air vent placement and noting concerns regarding drafts, poor window seals, cracks in the foundation and structural insufficiency which may be having an adverse effect on the temperature.

ELF (Extreme Low Frequency) is an environmental disturbance every investigator should take seriously. To understand why "infrasound" is so important to paranormal investigation, one must understand Vic Tandy's discovery in the early 1980's.

Tandy, a lecturer at Coventry University, theorized the frequency 19 hertz to be responsible for many ghost sightings. He was working late one night alone in the rumored "haunted" laboratory at Warwick, when he felt very anxious, then saw a gray blob out of the corner of his eye. When he turned to face it, there was nothing there.

The following day, he was working on a fencing foil with the handle in a vice. Although there was nothing touching it, it started to vibrate wildly. Being intrigued by these experiences, he decided to closely examine the events.

Further investigation led him to discover a recently installed fan emitting a frequency of 18.98 Hz, which is very close to the resonant frequency of an eye. The gray blob optical illusion was caused by the fan's similar infrasound frequency which in turn, resonated the eyeballs in his head.

In addition, he noted the desk holding the vice and fencing foil were placed in the center of the room. With the desk being of equal distance from all four walls and the fan running, the foil was exposed to a standing wave thus causing it to move and vibrate. Once the fan was shut down, the vibration ceased.

In today's world, human beings are exposed to excessive amounts of sound frequency due to technology, electronics, motors, etc. Like electromagnetic fields, extreme low frequencies can have numerous and debilitating effects on a client and their surroundings, similar to Tandy's experiences. By using an **oscilloscope**, an investigator should take ELF readings for each room. If a reading falls into the infrasound category, an investigator may want to examine their surroundings for electronics, motors, etc. which may be responsible for a standing wave length. An investigator may choose to shut down the suspected devices and observe the effects. If the experiment results in a change of sound frequency, it should be noted and the client should be informed of the findings.

The final phase is a **visual inspection** of the location looking for structural or foundational damage or gaps possibly caused by the location settling and/or a natural event, which could allow wild animals access into the property. We may find animal droppings, chew marks, holes in walls, or even half-eaten food left behind.

Flush toilets, run sink water and operate any other appliances which require running water to examine the effect water pressure has on the pipes. Inspect pipes and conduit to make sure they are properly secured. Loose water pipes can shake or rattle once changing water pressure is introduced.

One little known fact: If water pipes are touching electrical conduit which contains unshielded wiring, not only does the conduit carry a high EMF reading throughout the location, so does the water pipe, due to the water inside acting as a conductant.

Check the outside perimeter for tree limbs close to or on the roof and shrubbery which may be touching the walls or windows. Note window placement in correlation with streets and possible headlight infiltration. Have an investigator inside monitor a conversation outside to determine voice infiltration inside the location.

It is important to note any **safety issues** such as asbestos, low head room, tripping hazards, etc. and notify the team of their whereabouts.

While evaluating a piece of property, counter reference the client's claims against plausible causes. This may save a lot of time, effort and provide the client with much needed answers. **In order to test these causes thoroughly, reenactments must be conducted. If they prove to be successful, a display of the reenactment needs to be shown to the client.**

With so many variables and options to consider, a quick reference guide has been provided in the following pages.

Claims & Possible Causes

Moving shadows: Headlights through windows, mirror reflection, external illumination, candles.

Hearing voices: People talking outside, voices traveling through air vents, electronics, or toys.

Loud bangs: Water running through plumbing, duct work expansion, tree limbs.

Being watched, "the creeps": EMF sensitivity/ unshielded wiring, long exposure to electronics, fear cage exposure, ELF exposure.

Footsteps: pets/wild animals in walls or attic, settling support beams and joists, tree limbs.

Being touched: Cob webs, low hanging wire or string, drafts.

Moving objects: Traffic vibration, loose floorboards, ELF exposure.

Drapes and material being moved: Drafts, air vents, fans.

Knocking, tapping, scratching: Wild animals in walls or attic, tree limbs, ticking pilot light, plumbing/duct work expansion.

Visual apparition: Reflection, matrixing, (the mind playing tricks), pareidolia, apophenia.

Electronics going on and off/unplugged electronics turning on: Sleep mode settings, screen savers, alarms, batteries and alarm settings.

Flashes of light: Headlights, electronics, lightning, external illumination.

Just as paranormal claims need to be proven, so do these possible causes. Not everything is black and white or appears to be what it seems. Never assume, investigate.

FIVE

PROTECTION

Many investigators believe protection should be the first order of business before entering a suspected location. Although these rituals may be considered contradictory to an agnostic scientific approach, taking the time to address personal beliefs and asking the higher power of our choice for protection and guidance should not be, in any way, detrimental or have any bearing on that approach. Similar to separating church from state, these formalities are for personal reasons. Investigators should not implement personal faith into investigations, and keep final analysis of the case factual.

All religious faiths have some kind of prayers and rituals to protect against spiritual attachment. After all, most religious faiths and beliefs support some form of an afterlife and it is a belief in an alternative existence which brought us to this point in the first place. Since paranormal investigators are constantly submitting themselves to spiritually active locations, it only makes sense to take any available necessary precautions against spiritual attachment.

There are countless reasons why earthbound spirits would want to attach themselves to a human being. Some investigators believe these beings find comfort in reliving the physical aspects of life. Others may be confused and are attempting to contact the living for help. If this is the case, an investigator with equipment designed to communicate with them would make a perfect candidate. There is a possibility an entity may have personal reasons for an attachment ranging from admiration to malevolence. It is believed some deliberately seek out the living as an energy source, causing the person to be exhausted, less motivated, withdrawn and or cause health problems. This behavior is considered parasitical and malevolent in nature.

Anyway we look at it, attachments are never warranted and every precaution necessary should be taken to keep these appendages from occurring.

If protection against foreign energy invasion is necessary, first search ourselves and our own beliefs. Since beliefs are a major part of consciousness, one must find a faith or spirituality which best suits personal beliefs. Strengthening beliefs, strengthens consciousness thus providing the protection required. By developing a conscious energy immune system, our energy should be able to defend itself if an attachment is attempted. Theoretically in scientific terms, an electromagnetic field would be able to resist and fight off an invasion or manipulation from a foreign electromagnetic field.

There are numerous rituals and prayers from many different faiths which are used by those who choose to believe in their protective properties. It is up to each individual to decide which will work best for them. A personal favorite is a generic multi-denominational petition called;

The Investigators Prayer.

Divine Creator...Maker of all that is seen and unseen
We humbly ask for Your guidance and protection
In our quest for knowledge and understanding
We ask for Your direction and resolution
For ALL human energy existing in this domain
Both living and who have passed
We ask that You keep us free of attachment
From negative energy...malevolent spirits
And those who seek answers from the living...instead of
You
We humbly ask that You restore peace and harmony
To this dwelling and all its living occupants
And as always, we understand and appreciate
Your light surrounding us
Your love enfolding us
Your power protecting us
Your presence watching over us
Knowing...wherever we are...You are
And all is well. Amen

CHAPTER SIX

WITHOUT SCIENTIFIC EXPLANATION

Over half of the human population believe in ghosts. There are well over 100,000 paranormal investigators, ghost hunters, psychics, mediums, voodoo practitioners, religious leaders, witches and parapsychologists, ALL with varied beliefs and concepts regarding the afterlife, spirituality and the paranormal.

The dictionary term for paranormal is **"A claimed occurrence of an event or perception without scientific explanation...a supernatural phenomena."** Now even though this description is simple and vague, there are three key words which should draw attention, *without scientific explanation.* When used in context, they should be the basis for any paranormal investigation.

Cryptic beliefs should not be implemented nor unscientific tools and techniques used just because they have been employed for hundreds of years, or evidence presented which is unproven or excluding practical reason and common sense. There is already enough mysticism surrounding this field, which has splintered investigators into many off beat directions, impeding any scientific strides forward, and at times, turning this field of research into a punch line.

EXPLORING CONSCIOUS ENERGY

William Occam was a wise Franciscan Friar who devised the famous term Occam's Razor.

Occam's Razor-"The simplest explanation is usually the correct one."The principle states, if there are several possible reasons for something happening, **the reason which has the fewest assumptions is likely to be the correct one.**

As investigators of paranormal phenomena we often encounter unexplained and unusual events during the investigation or while reviewing evidence. But sometimes in our desire to find a good piece of evidence, our blinders go on and we tend to overlook logic to reach a paranormal conclusion, when the obvious answer is right in front of us. This is where we need to pause and check ourselves back into reality. If activity can be recreated by known artificial means, Occam's Razor has to conclude the recreation is more accurate than the assumptions of paranormal activity and misunderstandings or misinterpretations by the client.

The key significance of Occam's Razor, is to teach us to stop, think, and be realistic as to what is possible as opposed to being unlikely. Keeping an open mind is one thing, but if we have to connect too many dots and make too many assumptions to gain a paranormal answer, then more than likely it is not paranormal.

This leaves us with those three words, *without scientific explanation*, and a simple but not so easy, question to answer. Does the investigation scientifically support or denounce the existence of paranormal activity at the location?

CHAPTER SEVEN

THE PARANORMAL INVESTIGATION ORGANIZATION AND STRATEGY

L eading a scientifically based paranormal investigation requires a well thought out game plan. Properly placed equipment is vital in evidence recovery, however back up confirmation solidifies findings, strengthens the evidence captured and reduces the amount of assumption surrounding an event. By reducing assumption, we are applying Occam's Razor. By doing so, we are strengthening our scientific support of the event, as paranormal in nature.

When arriving at a location, we must consider all contamination possibilities and control it to the best of our ability. Consequently, we need to shut all windows and close all shades or blinds. If heating or air is running, it should be shut down if possible. Appliances and electronics which are not necessary should be turned off. If they are essential, they need to be noted and documented. In a perfect world, complete silence and eliminating external corruption are ideal conditions for an investigation.

If we are intending to set up a base within the location, it needs to be positioned in an area where visual and vocal contamination will not be an issue during the course of the investigation. Once base has been established, it is time to move on to strategic positioning of video, audio and detection devices.

Set up is all about documentation which is normally done through video, audio or photographic means. A good starting point would be the areas which we were not able to debunk. We must strategically place cameras and recorders in areas which have had reported activity **and have eluded a scientific explanation** through our preliminary analysis. These areas are considered **hot spots**.

Once our hot spots have been determined, cameras need to be distributed to these areas and camera angles need to be adjusted accordingly. If surveillance cameras with no audio capability are being used, voice recorders or a baby monitor should be strategically placed in that area to capture or monitor audio. If this is the circumstance, we will either need to simultaneously start the surveillance at the exact time as the voice recorders or time stamp the recorders once surveillance has started. This should synch the audio with the surveillance.

Now that we have everything in place, we need to once again consider the clients claims and what type(s) of detection devices are best suited to confirm that particular claim. The following example explains what our thought process should entail.

Example: A client's claim was of a moving shadow in the hallway. A moving shadow requires a moving light source and/or a moving object. If through our preliminary analysis, we were able to rule out reflection, another person or animal, candles, external illumination and headlight infiltration, then we can consider this *without scientific explanation*. It is from these deductions, we should consider the hallway a viable location to gather both documented proof and environmental readings of this moving shadow. In this example we have consulted our preliminary analysis and made a conscious decision to cover this specific area with video and audio. Once we have completed this task, we need to consider **back up confirmation**.

Since movement was involved, we should contemplate using a motion sensor with an alarm or a shadow detector plus a REM Pod or KII meter, in order to detect a stray EM field. Both pieces of equipment should be visible by the camera, so we not only capture the shadow, we can possibly capture the equipment's reaction to the event. The motion sensor or shadow detector **confirms** the movement and the REM Pod or KII **confirms** an energy source. If we are fortunate enough to capture video footage of the shadow, setting off a motion sensor, and an EMF detection device indicating an energy pulse, we have just documented and confirmed a paranormal event. Since shadows do not produce an energy signature, we have scientifically supported this assumption.

The same thought process and attention to detail should go into each and every strategic position covering a hot spot.

Final Preparations: Once initial set up is in place, a loosely designed schedule should be devised so each member of the team will have their turn. The team should be divided into small groups or pairs. Having a partner or two along makes monitoring equipment much easier, keeps teammates from getting rattled and provides a witness if anything should occur. One group should be monitoring base at all times. There should be walkie-talkie communication between base and group or groups in the field, allowing contact if anything is detected on surveillance. (A little known fact: walkie-talkies do set off certain EMF detectors. If spikes occur coincidentally with radio transmissions, it is a radio wave causing it.)

Each pairing should have a walkie talkie, an EMF detector, an IR Thermometer, a voice recorder for Real Time EVP sessions and or any other hand held detection devices and cameras which may provide added back up.

If more than one pairing or grouping is being sent in at a time, it is very important to keep them distanced from each other. The threat of contamination bleeding from one group into the other should always be considered when placing teams in strategic positions. If vocal or sound corruption becomes an issue, it is best to stop and remove one group from the equation, then send them in at a later time.

Approach and Intention: Our approach and intentions can directly affect the outcome of our investigation. We need to put ourselves in the right frame of mind, consider the circumstances and address our communication skills. Why is this so important? When attempting to establish communication with a human energy source, we need to respect the situation at hand and understand our predicament.

We are starting from ground zero, not knowing who or what we are dealing with. Therefore, they have the advantage of obscurity. Their whereabouts are not readily detected, which offers them the leverage of camouflage. With two counts against us, we are left with respectful maneuvers in an attempt to draw them out. This is where our understanding of human nature and basic manners come into play.

If a complete stranger walked into our home, asked who we were and why we were there, what kind of a response would we give them? Would it be favorable? If we did not want to be detected and someone started calling out our name, would we panic, run from this person or go deeper into hiding? If someone was pointing unusual devices in our general direction, would we be confused or afraid? Would we think it was a weapon? If someone was calling us names, using profanity, falsely accusing us of atrocities and making idle threats towards us, what would be our first course of action?

Many investigators make these mistakes and fore go any pleasantries in their approach. They seem to forget a human personality may be attached to the energy source they are addressing, then wonder why they are not getting a response. We believe, if there is a way to resolve a situation, especially in these circumstances, it's through communication. The best way to establish communication is through respect, manners, a kind word, an understanding of **their** situation and through an explanation of **our** intentions. By being cordial, it may open up a dialog.

These beings, for whatever reason, are making their presence known in an attempt to communicate and to be acknowledged. In these cases, reason may be intent. They may have unfinished business, someone to watch over, or a message they are trying to convey. They may be lost, confused or unaware they have passed on. They may be feeling a sense of abandonment, a fear of judgment or frightened of the unknown. They may be possessive and feel the property belongs to them. The list is endless, but if we can discover intention, it may possibly lead to resolution through diplomacy.

Last but not least, we should consider **their** view of the equipment we are operating. Let's face it, the gear we pull out of our cases are not standard household items. The way we hold devices in our hands, the lasers emitting beams of light, and even simple items such as a parabolic dish microphone and IR thermometers, could be mistaken as a weapon. We may be unknowingly pointing these devices in their direction. How would we react? We have to keep in mind people who lived in the 1800's on up to the 1950's would have no recollection or idea what this equipment is about.

We should do our best to explain each piece of equipment, what it is used for and if possible, demonstrate its functions in order to make them comfortable interacting with the devices.

Although this may sound petty we should consider that not only are we studying them, they may be studying us. If we take a good hard look at ourselves, doesn't it always come down to **trust**, before we open up to anyone?

CHAPTER EIGHT

THE PARANORMAL INVESTIGATION TECHNIQUES

As we contemplate which techniques and tests will be the most effective, our client's claims may provide an insight into approach, equipment and stimulus.

The most popular experiment is the EVP or Electronic Voice Phenomena session. This is an attempted one-sided interview conducted by the investigator which requires a voice recorder in record mode. The investigator asks questions directed toward the entity, in hopes of capturing a response on the recorder.

There are many theories surrounding the capture of these voices. With a lack of vocal cords, some believe these entities are manipulating the diaphragm in the microphone through ELF (extreme low frequency) sound resonance. Others presume the coil to be the effected source. One of the most compelling theory's would be that an entity's own electromagnetic field may be directly interacting with the electronics inside the voice recorder.

Since EVP sessions are currently one of the most effective ways to communicate, we need to understand the guidelines, techniques and proper approach behind conducting a successful one.

EVP Session: The first thing to remember is that **we want to hear their responses and/or reactions**. Therefore, we need the area to be as quiet as possible. Voice recorders are very sensitive so we need to keep our movement to a bare minimum and avoid our clothing from rubbing together. We need to control our breathing through our nose, by inhaling and exhaling as shallowly as possible. We **do not** hold the voice recorder in our hands, we place it on a sturdy surface. The slightest rub of our fingers on the recorder can resemble murmuring and whispers. When we ask questions, we speak in a normal inside voice. We **do not** lower our volume, mumble or **whisper**. Since entity's responses sometimes come off as whispers on a recording, **no one** should whisper during an EVP session, especially during discussions with other investigators.

There may be voice recorders left throughout the location which are recording ambient sound at each station. For these recorders, we need to announce the time, our presence and anyone else who has entered the room. This is called **stamping** and allows the reviewer to know who has entered the room and the time. When we leave the area, we should do the same. If we hear or have caused an audible disturbance, we should "**tag**" the recording by announcing what we heard or what caused the noise. In both instances, these simple procedures assist the reviewer by discrediting those disturbances.

Once we are ready to ask questions, we need to remember our goal–**get them talking and capture their responses**. Thus, questions need to be short and/or if possible broken into sections, leaving **four to eight second gaps** in between.

Using the recorder we have set aside for interview, we set the recorder down on a steady surface, hit the record button, announce the time and who is in the room. As we discussed in our approach, we should **start with a greeting, introductions and a brief description** of why we are visiting. This is considered **priming the conversation**.

Once the initial introductions have been completed, we should cut down our side of the conversation to a bare minimum with questions which are short, to the point, yet respectful and engaging, always leaving gaps in between for their responses.

Examples

"Are you okay? Is there something you need?"

"How can we help you?"

"May we deliver a message for you?"

"Who are you trying to contact?"

"Are you aware you have passed on?"

"May we ask...how did you die? When did you die?"

"Are you aware you are scaring this family? Is this your intention?"

"It's obvious you are seeking acknowledgment...do you wish to be noticed?"

"This equipment can provide you with a platform of recognition. A way to communicate. Is there something you need to say?"

Once we have completed our initial questioning we should do what is called a "real-time review," which is listening to the playback as soon as we are finished. If we capture intelligent responses, we will be able to redirect and possibly specify our approach the next go around. When we enter round two, we should stay focused on their answers and let them direct the conversation. By doing so, it may keep them talking by showing an interest in what they have to say. Showing compassion and concern for their side of the story is a positive psychological strategy which is used by many professionals to gather information from reluctant informants, patients, etc. Good cop without the bad cop.

The goal is to establish communication by keeping them engaged in a productive, non-combatant conversation.

More Audio Techniques (What else can we do with a voice recorder)

The **EVI** (Electronic Voice Interview) session is based on a theory which suggests conscious energy is able to hear and understand electronic voices much easier than physical voices. This experiment is relatively simple. All we have to do is prerecord approximately 20 questions on a voice recorder, leaving 10 second gaps in between. Place the recorder with the questions alongside a voice recorder that is set to record. Hit play for the questions and record on the other, then leave the room. Once the questioning has run its course, we need to check the results.

If an EVI becomes a second thought, we can always place a walkie talkie alongside a voice recorder set to record and ask the questions over the radio, basically giving us the same electronic source.

Another variation to the EVI may be through extraneous linguistics. If we are investigating a location where a foreign language was prevalent, we may want to conduct the exact same experiment, asking the questions in their foreign tongue. We may need assistance with this endeavor by prerecording someone who speaks the language and pronounces the words properly. Again, place the recorder alongside the other, start the foreign language interview and await the results.

Audio Triggers are an option many investigators seem to forget or forgo as a stimulus. They require thought out preparation in advance of the investigation, deliberately attempting to make an emotional connection with the property. For obvious audible reasons, **AT's should not be running throughout the investigation**, but 10-15 minutes in the background as a quiet mood setting may draw a reaction or two. We may want to consider music which has personal meaning, recorded sounds from a related workplace, dated radio or television broadcasts of historical events, recorded sounds of children laughing and playing or even the recorded voice of a loved one, to name a few.

When running AT's, make sure the volume is fairly low and away from any recording device. This will limit the amount of contamination from the trigger itself and make it possible to hear any verbal responses.

Trigger Objects can be anything which has a bearing on the case. Material items such as toys, jewelry, clothing, etc. are good, but if actual personal belongings are available, they should become a priority. Many investigators believe personal items which were cherished by someone long ago may be maintaining the energy of that person. Some of these items have been known to give off an EMF signature.

If we want to think outside of the box, trigger objects can include role play. We could read a personal letter out loud or a section of a diary. We could play a game which was preferred. We could imitate the sights and sounds of someone's workplace or hobby. If they had a passion for anything, addressing that passion may be beneficial in drawing them out.

As with all trigger objects, we should document the proceedings on video and audio, in order to capture any interaction or verbal response corresponding with the object or role play.

Equipment Interaction has its moments during an investigation. One of the most popular pieces of equipment to use is a **Flashlight**. This is done by taking a normal **Maglite** brand flashlight and barely twisting it to the off position. Set it down on any solid surface, possibly propping it against something so it won't roll away, and then step back. We may then ask yes or no questions by instructing the entity to turn it on if the answer is yes. For a more elaborate test we may wish to employ two or even three flashlights where we could designate one for yes and one for no, or even assign particular lights for certain answers. To possibly verify this interaction, we should be periodically change the wording of the questions or move the lights to different locations in the room. If the answers are the same, we may have legitimate interaction.

This same test can be conducted using **EMF detectors** which have digital displays. Many investigators prefer using KII Meters, but their accuracy is in doubt judging by their susceptibility to radio waves. A Mel Meter with a radiating antenna, a REM Pod or a Natural Tri-Field Meter with an alarm work best. Set the detector on any solid surface and step away. Ask the entity to approach or touch the device if the answer is yes or use two separate devices for yes and no answers.

Another form of equipment interaction can include our **IR Thermometer**. Since cold spots have often been attributed to paranormal activity it has been theorized, conscious energy may have a certain degree of control over the environment. Whether this hypothesis stands correct remains to be proven, yet the popular consensus among investigators points to an energy draw from the atmosphere causing substantial drops in temperature in an immediate area. To conduct this test, we set our thermometers on the ambient room setting and ask the entity to lower the temperature to a specific degree and wait for the results. If we wish to add a barometer to this equation, we may find it interesting to include barometric pressure readings.

As with all tests of this kind, we need to **document** on video the equipments reaction to this interaction. Otherwise, anything which may transpire undocumented remains a personal experience.

Traps-Not all cases require human interaction. In cases where activity occurs primarily in an empty location or does not surround anyone in particular, it is a good bet the entity may not wish to be discovered. It is in these circumstances we may find a less intrusive approach to be far more productive by backing the team off and allowing the equipment to do the work.

When setting up a trap investigation, it may be in our best interests to keep our discussion of ghosts, the claims in the location and our equipment's uses **out of any conversation in or around the property.** If we are dealing with intelligent conscious energy which is intentionally illusive, there is a strong possibility **our conversations are being heard**. However, invading their space, placing unknown gadgets all over **without explanation**, may peak their curiosity enough to draw them out into the open once we have left. This psychological maneuver is designed to appeal to a human's natural inquisitive mind set.

Once we have strategically covered the location in surveillance and audio, we can turn our attention towards detection such as motion sensors, EMF detectors, Geophones, shadow detectors and if necessary, laser grids to enhance our video footage. It is imperative to have **ALL** detection devices on camera to document their reactions.

If trigger objects are being used, they must be placed in camera view, preferably alongside a detection device. If audio triggers are being used they should be kept short and played at the beginning of the trap to eliminate contamination concerns.

If EMF data loggers are available, we should tactically place them in key positions to record spikes. If more than one is at our disposal, we may set them in sequence down a well traveled area to determine movement and direction.

Hunter trap cameras are perfect for hard to reach areas where surveillance or cabling could be an issue. Additional external IR illumination may be needed to assist the sensor, if placed in extremely dark environments.

Once our trap has been set, recording should start, the location shut down and all living beings vacated from the premises.

Trigger Trap-If we are using a trigger object which has been rumored to move on its own, we may want to place the item in an open area and mark its original placement, by setting it on top of a light dusting of flour or a piece of paper which has the object's position outlined with a circle.

As with all traps, surveillance is essential in capturing the event as it is taking place, thus legitimizing the event's authenticity.

Environmental Readings-Even though environmental readings are not as sexy as EVP's and video evidence, we should always be aware of these readings in correlation with conscious energy. It is vital for the advancement of technology and may widen our spectrum of understanding in regard to the scientific make up of such energy.

Starting with the Electromagnetic Field, we should always have an **EMF Detector** at our side. An EMF detector measures in milligauss (mg) units with a range of 0mg to 188mg and a reach of up to eight feet away. Normal base readings for most locations are from 0mg to 3.0mg due to electronics and wiring. It is important to know these base readings **BEFORE** using these devices as a tool to determine activity. (See Preliminary Investigation)

When exploring EMF disturbances we need to move slowly and definitively, holding the detector out where we can view the changes. Once a spike occurs, we should come to a complete stop and wait to see if the spike dissipates or holds its reading. If it holds, move slowly in all directions to determine circumference, height and width. If it holds and is traceable back to a wall, an electronic device or an appliance, this should be noted and cross referenced with the preliminary findings. If it dissipates, move slowly from side to side in an attempt to recapture its position. What we are looking for is EMF strength, its maneuverability and it's non-association with man-made components. This would be considered a stray and moving EMF which is normally attributed with the existence of conscious energy.

Many clients have claims of cold spots. It is believed, when an entity draws energy from the environment it causes a significant drop in temperature within the immediate area which is noticeable to human touch. This is why many investigators insist on having an **IR Thermometer** on hand. These thermometers provide both ambient room temperature readings and laser point to take readings from one specific area. As with all environmental equipment, slow steady movement is required to allow the device to take accurate readings.

It has long been rumored that barometric pressure can be effected by paranormal activity. The unit of measurement for barometric pressure is in millibars (mb). If there is a localized increase or decrease of 20mb, this can be considered unusual. Many scientifically based investigators put a lot of stock in barometric readings and use a **barometer** in correspondence with an EMF detector for back up confirmation.

Compatible with a barometer and EMF detector is the **air ion counter** which is a hand held meter designed to measure ion density or the number of ions per cubic centimeter in an immediate environment. It can measure positive or negative ions separately or both simultaneously. In theory, conscious energy requires an energy draw from the environment. Many believe this is done by extracting either positive or negative ions out of the atmosphere in order to manifest or perform a task. An ion is an atom, group of atoms, or molecule which has acquired a net electric charge by pulling electrons in or dispensing electrons from an initial electrical neutral configuration. Hypothetically, if an entity can manipulate an

57

electron pull or release, we should be able to gather a reading of this significant change in the ion count within the immediate area.

These alterations in the ion count can also produce static electricity due to the high ratio of positive ions changing to negative ions. Many investigators have heard loud pops and cracks during investigations which many attribute to a static electrical charge. If we continue

to pursue this line of thinking, we must consider the use of a **Digital Electro-Static Meter**. These meters are designed to detect and measure static electrical charges up to four feet away. The range on these devices is from +/- 0.00kv/inch to +/-19.99kV/inch with the unit of measurement being kilovolts per inch. It is theorized, the static electrical reading surrounding paranormal activity is +/-5kV/inch from the base reading of the location.

These devices, when used in concert with one another, are excellent resources for back up readings and provide us with expanded details surrounding these environmental disturbances.

Collecting and documenting these environmental readings may one day provide an insight into the nuts and bolts of conscious energy. By documenting these energy signatures and presenting a direct correlation with paranormal activity, we may be able to piece together a common denominator, which may one day produce a scientific equation for this phenomena.

Personal Experiences-There is a chance during the course of the investigation, an event may occur which will not be captured on audio or video. Even though there may have been witnesses, these are referred to as **personal experiences** due to their **lack of documentation**. Many an investigator can describe the situation where a piece of visual evidence was just off camera or occurred in an area which was not covered. Some investigators believe intelligent spirits do this intentionally in a display of disapproval or to lead the investigation in a distinct direction. Needless to say, even an **undocumented** full bodied apparition appearance viewed by many witnesses is still "the one that got away."

However, personal experiences do have merit. These experiences may be leading investigators towards an area or item in the location, or be informing the team of its intent. Therefore, these occurrences shouldn't be taken lightly and a team should be prepared to make on the fly changes in strategy. These changes in video surveillance, audio and location of detection devices should be done quickly and according to the occurrence's whereabouts.

All personal experiences should be investigated immediately. If audible activity occurs which is not seen, we must make an attempt to trace the sound to its origins. If an object has been noticeably moved, we need to consider a logical explanation first. By rewinding surveillance, we may discover a possible culprit. By reviewing audio, we may hear the event more clearly, possibly exposing an alternate explanation. We should take environmental readings of the object for any lingering energy levels or unusual temperature distinctions. Always run tests and re-enactments which follow a protocol for rational reason **before** coming to a paranormal conclusion.

If visual activity is being witnessed, it must be investigated immediately. For example, if a shadow appears in a room, we should approach the shadow and make an attempt to discover a logical source for its appearance. If it was moving, we should look outside for headlights or a source of reflection. If it is still, we should make an attempt to discover a light source which may be casting the shadow. Obviously, if we are unable to find the origin of its appearance or the shadow eludes our advances, we need to gather temperature and EMF readings during its manifestation. Although the occurrence may be awe inspiring, it is no time to sit back and become a spectator. Even if the occurrence has come and gone, we should look into all environmental aspects surrounding the appearance. These occurrences sometimes leave an energy trail or temperature change in their wake, therefore an attempt to gather these readings should be done as quickly as possible.

Sometimes, a personal experience can be more personal than we would like. Physical contact is one of the most reported personal experiences made by clients and investigators. Many of the reports range from light touching to marks or scratches on the body. However, as in all personal experiences, we should look into logical attributes first. If we are in poorly lit or dark locations, we should turn on the lights or flashlight and examine where the occurrence took place. We should first inspect the area on the person which was touched. If no marks are readily visible, we should then inspect the area they were in. Low hanging objects such as pull strings for lights, cob webs, etc. are obvious culprits, but we shouldn't rule out a draft or breeze.

If scratches or marks are appearing followed by a burning sensation, we must first consider where this person was to receive such an injury. Scratches and rashes can be caused by bumping into something abrasive or leaning up against something which may have caused an allergic reaction. There is always a possibility they were bitten by a spider or other insect. If none of these alternatives seem to match or adhere to the injury, we should take an EMF reading of the injury and document it on video or photo. Obviously, apply first aid if needed.

Another form of personal contact is through our psyche. There have been instances where a client or an investigator have been overwhelmed with a surge of emotion such as sadness or anger which were not relevant at the time. In these circumstances, the emotions come out of nowhere and are not self warranted. It is believed the person is experiencing emotions brought on by an outside influence. If anyone appears to be displaying these symptoms, it is advised to remove the person from the immediate area and take a break. Usually a breath of fresh air and a glass of water will relieve the tension accompanying these episodes.

As with all documented, undocumented and personal experiences, an immediate and thorough examination of the occurrence is necessary.

Controlling Our Emotions: It is in our human psyche to get startled. It is no different than unexpectedly running into someone around a corner. However, there are going to be times when we will be galvanized, which may make our hair stand on end and our heart rate go up. It is what we do after the initial shock which will determine our resolve and professionalism.

Controlling our emotions can be a test of will. However, if our rational thought process has been compromised due to an occurrence and we are finding ourselves unable to contribute, we must do the professional thing and remove ourselves **quietly** from the situation. A client does not need to view a visual and audible display of fear to further feed their imagination.

CHAPTER NINE

ANALYSIS AND REVIEW

In our quest to capture evidence, some investigators have been known to be less than thorough in their determinations.(I'm being kind here.) Our thirst for evidence and our imagination should **never** be involved in the analysis process. It is just as important for us to be agnostic in review as it is during the first two phases of the investigation.

When reviewing audio, video, surveillance, and photographs, it is important to have a quiet and uninterrupted area to do it in. Distractions could cause us to miss something. If fatigue starts to set in, we should to take a break until we have improved our cognizance.

As we initially go over our audio, video and surveillance, we need to note any and all readily unexplained events. A list should be compiled, documenting time and a brief description. This makes locating these events easier during the review board presentation.

Review Board: Each team should conduct a review board assembly for each case, going over the suspected events captured on audio, video and in photographs. This provides variety in opinion and alternative explanations, which may have been overlooked by the initial reviewing member. If a piece of evidence acquires too many explanations, assumptions, or fails to meet the board's criteria, the event must be considered null and void. However, if an event lacks premise, produces more questions than answers, and has the assembly scratching their heads, the occurrence should be given the go ahead for a test of its authenticity.

Burden of Proof and Re-Creation: If potential evidence has passed review board standards, our preemptive measures should include a rigorous step by step follow up, in an attempt to debunk the occurrence through rational means and re-creation.

We should cross reference video with audio, in an effort to uncover human, animal or man-made interference. We should be checking surveillance, establishing everyone's whereabouts by collecting an accurate head count of our teammates and anyone else at the location. We should review our preliminary findings for any feasible contributions.

If a visual anomaly has been captured, a reenactment must be considered. This may require us to return to the location in order to test various potential causes, leaving nothing to chance. Justifications which may have been previously overlooked, may eventually be staring us in the face upon our reassessment of the location. We must be diligent in our efforts to replicate the occurrence, by all means necessary.

It is our burden to prove the occurrence anything but paranormal in nature. If we have taken into account all matter of reason, we are left with no explanations and the event stands on its own merit, **then** we may consider it a potential indicator of paranormal activity.

CHAPTER TEN

REVEALING EVIDENCE TO A CLIENT

A s with the entire process of an investigation, the client's concerns should be our top priority. Even though we may be ecstatic over the potential evidence captured, a client may **not** be so enthused. We must consider their position, by reminding ourselves this person has to live and or work in these conditions. Co-habitation with this phenomena is not always a well received conclusion.

It is best to break the news gently but factually. It's advisable to start by asking the client if there have been any occurrences since the investigation. If so, they should be duly noted.

Proceeding with the reveal, we should notify the client of our preliminary findings which provide logical explanation. If the client fails to understand this reasoning, we should literally demonstrate our hypothesis by showing them environmental readings, pointing out evident contributors and or reenacting their claim in the alternative manner.

Once we have covered these aspects, we can move on to claims and occurrences which have numerous assumptions **outside** of paranormal description. Even though these assumptions may not be tested, the client needs to be made aware of their possibilities.

Finally, we can proceed with the evidence which shows signs of paranormal assumption. It is imperative to remain factual and to the point in this stage of presentation. We must **not** include personal opinion (even if asked for it), religious beliefs or theoretical descriptions when presenting this kind of evidence to a client. Evidence must be proposed in a vague and pure form.

Example: "Unexplained shadow movement was captured in the northeast bedroom at approximately 11:23 p.m. We were able to rule out any team members, headlight infiltration or any other practical source to this occurrence."

If EVP's are included in the reveal, they should **not** be deciphered for the client.

Example: "What appears to be a voice, was captured at 9:43 p.m. in the living room. We can confirm this voice does not belong to any member of the team or others present at the time."

If the client chooses to interpret words from these recordings, this is their prerogative. If the team agrees with the client, this can be considered back up confirmation, which **then** can be conveyed to the client. However, it is not advisable to interpret entire sentences out of a few audible words. This can lead to a message or intention being misconstrued.

Being vague and unbiased in our presentation should not be considered disconcerting or cold. On the contrary, we are allowing the client to draw their own conclusions. Misinterpreting audio messages, applying unsubstantiated identity to beings we do not know, and misappropriating paranormal theory to environmental readings is deceitful and shows lack of respect for the client and our own integrity. By conducting a factually based presentation of the evidence, we are remaining true to the client and ourselves.

CHAPTER ELEVEN

COUNSELING

If a location shows signs of legitimate activity, it's a safe bet the client will ask for advice and or further assistance. This is where an investigator can find themselves in the gray area between practical application and supernatural theory.

If we are uncomfortable or feel unqualified with meeting the client's request, it is in the client's and our best interest to forward their concerns to an outside authority who may be more qualified addressing these matters.

When deciding on a suitable candidate, we should be looking for those with successful reputations who have acquired years of experience and favorable results. Many teams prefer utilizing psychics or sensitives, who may be able to communicate with the entity through remote viewing or a physical evaluation of the property. Although these tactics have never been scientifically proven, some of these specialists have surprisingly decent success rates. In some instances, psychic intervention has actually lowered activity levels in a location. If it works, it works.

EXPLORING CONSCIOUS ENERGY

Numerous teams favor clergymen or clergywomen who conduct location cleansing and blessings. These religious advocates specialize in spiritual intervention, providing counsel for both the client and the entity in question, similar to a spiritual mediator. Their origins of faith span all walks of religion and spirituality. If we are considering introducing an individual with these credentials into the equation, we must first consult the client and allow them to decide if this course of action is acceptable and if so, choose the religion, faith or belief of their choice.

When teams find themselves over their head in an investigation, a team with more experience is always an option. Again, success rate and results should be considered. There is no shame in admitting a case may be more trouble than we can handle. Sometimes a different perspective or approach can change everything. Keep in mind, this is about the client, not our pride.

If neither one of these options are satisfactory with the client, we may be lured into providing a rough synopsis. If we are placed in this situation following the reveal, it is advised to request a deferral, until we can conduct research and explore the options available. It is in this moment of pause that we should continue to seek advice from extraneous sources, research results from similar cases and further study the conditions surrounding our client's troubles. It is at this point we must remain factual and focused on the literal description of each occurrence.

If an occurrence continues to have the potential of being written off by rational means, **it should not be included in the speculation process**. (Occam's Razor) These events can quickly become a slippery slope and need to be grounded in fact, **not paranormal conjecture**. These facts need to be reaffirmed with the client, so there are no misunderstandings regarding alternative contributions.

Ruling out events with secondary explanation, we may be left with activity and claims which we were unable to debunk and defy logical description. This is where we need to allow the events to speak for themselves, preventing our own assumptions from dictating motive.

Our research should encompass a re-evaluation of the occurrences. Do these events appear to be malevolent or benevolent? Are they singling out one person? Does the phenomena coincide with renovations or other changes in or to the household? Do the occurrences correspond with the introduction of an item, artifact, or family heirloom? Is the activity interactive with the living? Has this activity followed the client from location to location?

Again, attributing circumstances may need to be considered. Changes in a client's lifestyle have been theorized to stir up activity. Were there any additions to the family? Was a pet introduced to the location? Was there a recent death of a loved one? Is anyone experimenting with things they shouldn't be? Is anyone going through physical or emotional trauma? Is there distress in the home? Is the client voluntarily welcoming these events?

Conscious energy is human energy. It has intelligence and personality, thus displaying human traits. However, in these cases, not everything is what it appears to be. A visual appearance could be anything from a visitation of a loved one to a deliberate scare tactic. A disembodied voice can be a message or a warning. Audible disturbances can be residual or a call for attention. How a client perceives their experiences may not reciprocate the entity's intentions. Therefore, **motive should be left out** of the speculation process.

Seven Day Study:

This leaves us with methods which are strictly experimental, in an attempt to observe reaction. Tests of this magnitude can produce varied results, ranging from a decrease in activity to a significant increase in intensity. With the client(s) being physically, and in some way, emotionally connected to the situation, their involvement is mandatory. Thus, the client needs to be aware of the ramifications and possible drawbacks at stake, **requiring them to provide us with written approval** for the study. With their blessing, we will then need to prep them for a week long research project, which will attempt to document reaction to client interaction.

These tests will primarily be a series of 30 minute one-on-one EVP sessions, which should include various members of the household or business. They need to be conducted at least once a day at various times and if possible 2 to 3 times daily. Questions and interrogation tactics should be varied and predetermined in advance, according to previous claims, occurrences and the person asking the questions. During these half hour sessions, the interviewer needs to be alone in the room, under camcorder surveillance covering the immediate area. During the one-on-ones, it is imperative for the location to be as quiet as possible.

With the one-on-ones being mandatory, there are possible strategic experiments the client can perform over this week long study. By judging the subtle hints from the evidence captured, surrounding circumstances, and convincing behavioral patterns, we may be able to come up with some creative, yet productive tests.

71

If a loved one is believed to be the source of the activity, both material and audio triggers should be taken into consideration. Items which may have belonged to and or cherished by the deceased should be brought out and placed in camera view beside the person conducting the session. Songs or familiar sounds which have meaning can be briefly played prior to the session, in order to stir emotion. The interviewer may choose to read aloud a love letter or verbally recollect a story from days gone by. With the countless options available, this type of experiment should be strategically thought out in advance, with audio stimulation immediately preceding the one-on-one sessions, but **not** during.

If a physical object was introduced into the location which appears to coincide with the activity, we should have the client remove the item for a day or two in an attempt to determine its significance to the case. After this time period has passed, a reintroduction of the object should be made to delineate it's contributions, if any.

If the activity appears to be focused around a single individual, the one-on-one sessions should be conducted solely by this person for the first 3 days. On the 3rd day, the individual should progressively spend less time in the location as the week moves forward, with the last day being completely truant. In this person's absence, other members of the household or business should continue the scheduled one-on-one sessions in hopes of determining any changes or lowered levels of interaction and communication.

If renovations or changes to the location are under suspicion, it may be productive to conduct EVP sessions while the work is in process, taking 10 minute breaks to ask questions. These breaks will require a quiet environment in order to capture responses. It is therefore suggested all machinery and tools which produce sound be silenced during these pauses.

Throughout the week, there may be a chance of increased activity which can be a derivative of enhanced interaction. With acknowledgment comes possible reciprocation. Although it may appear to be malevolent at first, assumptions need to be set aside. If these outbursts occur, it will then be in the client's best interests to stop what they are doing and conduct an EVP session at that moment. Shortly after these events, there may be a small window of opportunity to establish communication while the entity is craving recognition. Clients should document the occurrence(s) for further analysis, including time, who was involved and what led up to the event(s).

Sometime during their seven day trial, a client may want to consider a meeting of the minds. This type of interaction can produce mixed results, some of which are not favorable. It will be the client's decision to induce this tactic and they should be warned in advance of its ramifications. This maneuver is considered an attempt to reason with the entity, as opposed to asking questions. If not done properly, it can be mistaken as provoking and demanding. It is therefore advised to discuss these verbal intentions with the team and predetermine the content in advance. Again, the client must respect the situation they are in. These requests should be presented in a diplomatic format. **Negotiations which include idle threats and provocation are strongly ill advised.** These appeals need to come across as considerate and respectful. In turn, the client should ask for the same consideration. The client may choose to tactfully negotiate a truce, which involves guidelines for co-habitation. Compassion for the entity's well being and genuine consideration will prove to be beneficial in this tactical stage.

As with all interaction during this week-long endeavor, this type of diplomatic intervention must be documented on camera and audio for further analysis. Once the week is over, the equipment and all of the recorded data needs to be returned to the team for review.

Counseling a client is never easy and varies from location to location. However, respect and compassion for their situation is always welcome. Sometimes, just being there for them, and putting our best foot forward, is enough.

CHAPTER TWELVE

CLEANSING A LOCATION

The time may come when a client will ask for a house cleansing. Although this ritual has never been scientifically proven to work, we have to remember our work is affiliated with metaphysical study. Thus, if we have provided conclusive evidence indicating paranormal activity in a client's home or business, we have done our job. What a client chooses to do with that information is strictly on their shoulders. It is therefore suggested anything which can empower the client, strengthen **(not influence)** their beliefs, and allow them to build up their own conscious immunity, may be a step in the right direction.

Even though we may have investigative brothers and sisters who find this ritual to be trivial, the truth of the matter is, it doesn't matter. At this point, the ball is in the client's hands. It is up to their faith, their will and their resolve. All we can do is provide them with the information.

White Sage Bundles

For centuries, white sage has been held sacred in many religions due to its effective purifying energies. The botanical name for this herb is Salvia. This small evergreen shrub has been used in herbal medicine due to its antibiotic, antifungal, and antispasmodic properties. It has been used for thousands of years in a ritualistic ceremony called smudging. The effectiveness of smudging is based on a theory. The hypothesis suggests the smoke is capable of attaching itself to negative energy or spirits. As it clears, it takes the negative energy with it. A standard smudging ceremony is very simple. It is suggested the location to be quiet and peaceful, with little to no interruptions. According to belief, the client must be in a receptive and intentional state of mind, **for they will be the one performing the ceremony**. Once the client has mentally prepared themselves and the location, the ritual can begin.

The actual ceremony starts by lighting a bundle of white sage with a lighter or match, letting it burn for a few seconds, then blowing out the flame, allowing the smoke to build. **(Safety Concern**: Be aware of material, clothing, hair and flammables when maneuvering the smudge bowl throughout the location.)

White Sage Burning in Bowl

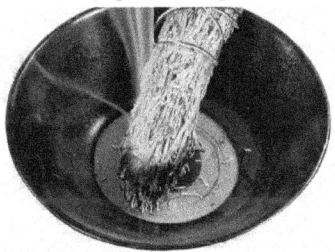

It is customary to start at the lowest point of the dwelling and work upward throughout the location. This technique suggests as the smoke permeates and ascends from each room, it is driving out all negative energy, room by room and level by level.

This is done by carefully carrying the smoking smudge bowl into each room, closet and crevasse, fanning the smoke into each corner, allowing it's incense to completely engulf the immediate area. It is recommended the client have a lighter or matches with them at all times during the process, as it is considered ill-fated to allow the sage to burn out before the entire home can be cleansed.

Many cleansing experts believe a prayer should be said as the smudging is underway. This should be up to the client's discretion, beliefs or religious convictions. If they don't have any one in particular, a standard heartfelt prayer may be said, such as **"May Peace, Love and Light come into this home and upon all who live here."** If a client is compelled to use Holy Water, it should be sprinkled throughout each room, along with a prayer of their choice.

After the entire location has been smudged, it is then suggested to allow the sage bundle to burn out on its own,

77

preferably in a central location of the home. Once the bundle ceases to burn, it is advised to take a pinch of ash from the bowl and place it above each opening, leading in and out of the house, along with a short prayer. If a client chooses to use Holy Water, this same procedure can be done in the same manner.

To complete the ritual, it is recommended to thank the powers called upon for cleansing the space, then verbally declaring the location to be filled with light, love and happiness.

CHAPTER THIRTEEN

INVESTIGATIVE & PARANORMAL

Theory

Battery Draw: It has been speculated an entity can draw energy from almost any source, including the batteries in our equipment. Many investigators make it a habit to use fresh and recharged batteries on each investigation, then noting sudden and drastic battery drain, if it occurs. Some investigators believe this is done intentionally, to sabotage the equipment. (Side Note: Camcorders using a flip out screen drain batteries quicker when the screen is in use.)

Energy Supply: Locations which have high man-made EMF levels have long been suspected of being an activity feeding ground. Although it has never been proven, it has been theorized conscious energy requires a source to draw from. If this is the case, a location with these qualifications would certainly meet supply and demand.

Cold Spots: Believed to be the by-product of an entity drawing energy from an immediate area. This may be caused by an entity accumulating or attracting negative ions from the air, producing a concentrated high pressure bubble, thus lowering the temperature. These readings should be detectable on an ion counter, barometer and IR thermometer.

Renovation and Change: It's a common belief renovations and or changes, in or to a location, can stir up activity, when change is not acceptable by all "inhabitants." Changes such as, a new baby, an adopted pet, a new roommate, as well as renovations, second hand items, antiques, furniture, or even an alteration in paint color, have all been theorized to coincide with escalated paranormal activity at one time or another.

Animal Sensitivity: Animals are believed to be ultra-sensitive to spirits and paranormal occurrences. Some say it is their heightened awareness to EMF radiation which allows them to pick up on an entity's location. Others believe their sight is far more advanced than ours, which offers a capability to see further into the UV and IR spectrum.

The Middle Ground: Is the existence believed to be in between our physical being and where our consciousness is supposed to go. (Into the light) This controversial state is supposedly where lost spirits are trapped, for whatever reason, until they find their way or their work on Earth is done.

Demonic VS. Negative Energy: Many religious sanctions believe in demonic spirits, even though they state a demonic appearance is very rare. I have been told demons use lost receptive souls to do their bidding. My personal opinion is that evil exists in each and every one of us. Some of us control it better than others, making us decent human beings. Judging by what I know of human nature, I stand by the theory, "If they

80

were a jerk in life, they will probably be a jerk in death," thus explaining negative energy and behavior.

Intention and Occurrences: Apparition and shadow appearances can be very frightening. Disembodied voices, objects being moved, unexplained noises are all startling and unnerving. What if they are not intended to be? It has been my experience, intention is overlooked, and many times, misinterpreted. One theory suggests conscious energy has limited control over their appearance or actions in the physical world. It may require a vast amount of effort and energy on their part just to make their presence known. If this is so, what appears to be a deliberate attempt to scare someone may be a simple request for recognition.

Reincarnation and Past Life Experiences: If Einstein's theory of conservative energy proves correct and is applicable to conscious energy, the sum of all energy in the system must remain consistent. If so, this could explain past life experiences. If we truly are reconstituted through the system and back into an entirely different physical existence, it could justify previous memories surfacing at some point.

Subconscious Visitation: Since our brain is most active while we are asleep, our subconscious state has long been considered an ideal stage for visitation. There have been numerous reports of loved and not so loved ones making appearances during REM sleep. If electromagnetic fields can truly alter and effect other fields, it would make sense to contact us while our brain is most receptive.

Apparitions and Shadow People: Theory speculates disembodied masses of consciousness are capable of manifesting themselves by drawing ionized atoms from the atmosphere into an organized accumulative mass, which can reflect light or project an image. Hypothetically, it is similar to a camera rasterizing pixels, then synchronizing them into a composite video signal or television air wave.

Related Definitions

Agnostic: One who is doubtful or noncommittal about something.

Apophenia: The human tendency to seek pattern in random shapes and information.

Apparition: A visual appearance of a deceased person or animal.

Back Up Confirmation: evidence captured by two or more pieces of equipment

Benevolent: Caring, kind, friendly

Claim: What is reported to investigators by the client.

Co-habitation: When a client accepts, lives and or works in an active location.

Cold Spot: A defined area of intense cold which is considerably cooler than its surroundings.

Debunk: When an investigator can apply a non-paranormal explanation for a reported claim.

Demonic: Believed to be a non-human spirit, usually associated with negative energy which has fallen out of favor with a higher power—an evil presence.

Disembodied Voice: A voice which can be physically heard, not attributed to audio devices or a physical being.

Document: The use of surveillance and video cameras, voice recorders, and still photos to certify evidence.

EMF-Electromagnetic Field: The fields of energy surrounding electric wires, power lines electronics, and other current-carrying devices.

Energy Trail: The residual EM trace, following a paranormal event.

Entity: A generic term used to describe ghosts, spirits, non-human spirits etc.

EVP-Electronic Voice Phenomena: Unexplained voices captured on voice recorders which were **not heard** or produced by a living being.

Fear Cage: A term used to describe an area with very high EMF readings caused by poor wiring, electronics or appliances.

Going Green: The nickname for turning out the lights and starting the investigation in night vision.

Hot Spot: An area in a location which has been rumored to be active and defies all debunking attempts.

Intelligent Haunt: An entity which is capable of interacting with human beings, either verbally and or physically.

IR (Infrared): Infrared light is located in between visible light and the microwave portions of the electromagnetic spectrum. IR light provides night vision for surveillance.

Infrasound: A wave phenomena sharing the physical nature of sound but with a range of frequencies below that of human hearing. Usually under 20Hz.

Malevolent: Malicious, destructive, dangerous.

Manifestation: The act of conscious energy attempting to make a visual appearance or cause an occurrence.

Matrixing: When the mind attempts to make sense of an occurrence, convincing the person of its authenticity.

Metaphysical: speculative or abstract reasoning, highly theoretical.

Negative Energy: a hostile and unpleasant spirit with the possibility of becoming malevolent.

Non-Human Spirit: An entity which is not the result of a physical being living on Earth. This category includes angels, elementals, etc.

Occam's Razor: "The simplest explanation is usually the correct one," alluding to the reason which has the fewest assumptions likely being the correct one.

One-on-One Session: When a client conducts an EVP session on their own, alone in the location.

Orb: A video or photographic effect caused by night vision or a flash reflecting off moisture in the air, dust particles, flying insects, etc. (Refer to Occam's Razor)

Paranormal: Events above the normal or everyday experience. Events which cannot be readily explained by known conventional reason or commonly accepted science.

Pareidolia: The imagined perception of a pattern or meaning where it does not actually exist.

Personal Experience: An encounter which is experienced by a client or investigator which is not or cannot be documented.

Poltergeist: A human beings capability to telekinetically move objects unknowingly and subconsciously.

Possession: Believed to be what happens when a spirit or non-human energy has mentally taken over a physical being.

Private Investigation: An investigation conducted for a private individual, with the sole purpose of helping the individual.

Provocation: An ill-advised intimidating technique, to get an entity to interact.

Re-creation: An experimental reenactment, in an attempt to debunk an occurrence.

Remote Viewing: the act of a sensitive, to extract information from an external location or entity, through teleportation.

Residual Haunt: An energy imprint of a past event which replays over and over again like a video recording. Therefore, it is not an actual haunting.

Sensitive: a generic term for psychic or medium.

Shadow Figure: A dark human-form manifestation which has no definition other than its outline and solid dense appearance.

Smudging: The ritualistic act of burning white sage during a house cleansing ceremony.

Spiritual Attachment: The act of an entity following and attaching itself to a human being.

Stamping: When investigators announce their name and time, as they enter or leave a room.

Stray EMF: An EM field which has no man-made source or origin.

Tagging: When investigators verbally report something they have heard or witnessed during an EVP session.

Telekinesis: The ability to manipulate physical objects using the body's static electrical charges. Considered a psychic extension of a physical being.

Trigger Object: A physical object used to stimulate a paranormal event.

Ultraviolet (UV): Ultraviolet is located in the upper end of the electromagnetic spectrum. As with Infrared light, UV light is not visible to the naked eye.

Vortex: Considered a momentary doorway or portal which allows entities and other paranormal phenomena to enter into our state of existence.

White Noise: White noise is random indefinable static sound which covers and combines all wavelengths and frequencies.

ABOUT THE AUTHOR

B rian Kent is the founder and lead investigator of Paracon Investigations. The team is based out of Omaha, Nebraska and has been in existence since 2007. Brian's passionate interest in the paranormal started at a young age when his parents unknowingly moved the family into a house which had considerable paranormal activity.

Since then, he has researched this phenomena for almost twenty years and conducted paranormal investigations for more than a decade.

He has written a thesis, "The Theory of Conscious Energy," and "The House On Lincoln Street," which is about his childhood in an active home.

Brian has been a guest speaker at high schools, colleges, and universities throughout Nebraska, hoping to educate and illuminate those who wish to understand the cause and effects surrounding paranormal phenomena.

Along with Paracon, Brian and his team conduct paranormal investigative classes throughout the year, offering basic instruction in equipment, techniques, location evaluation, debunking, and replication. Following these classes, students are led on an investigation, allowing them to apply what they have learned.

He has appeared on numerous internet radio programs including, "Spiritual Spectrum," with Michka Grant, "Live Paranormal," with Michelle Fitzpatrick, and Dead Air Radio's, "Club Para," with Ryleigh Black.

ACKNOWLEDGEMENTS

*This book is dedicated to my teammates in **Paracon** for their support. **Lisa Kovanda** for her inspiration and guidance through the writing process. **Julie Hagemeier** for her editing talent. **Alicia Mattern** for her artistic talent. And to each and every one of you who have had paranormal experiences.*

www.ingramcontent.com/pod-product-compliance
Lightning Source LLC
Chambersburg PA
CBHW070757290526
45795CB00002B/581